For

The Road to Friendship

Compiled by Kiyana Sakena Horton

Illustrated by Barbara Chiantia

PETER PAUPER PRESS, INC.
WHITE PLAINS, NEW YORK

For Kim A.

Book design by Arlene Greco

Illustrations copyright © 1998
Barbara Chiantia
Licensed by Wild Apple Licensing

Text copyright © 1998
Peter Pauper Press, Inc.
202 Mamaroneck Avenue
White Plains, NY 10601
ISBN 0-88088-102-X
Printed in China
7 6 5 4 3 2 1

The Road to Friendship

Contents

Introduction

The road to friendship is life's most rewarding path. Although the road that you travel may have bends, curves, ruts, and gullies, friendship will provide direction as you proceed, and comfort at life's many way stations. The road to friendship, when traveled by people with hearts and intentions that are true, does indeed go on forever.

THE EDITORS

Build and Grow
As You Go

You can lay the foundation of a
friendship in a matter of
moments, but it is a work of
time to build a monument.

MADELYN WATT

Love, to endure life's sorrow
and earth's woe, needs friendship's solid masonry below.

ELLA WHEELER WILCOX

Familiarity breeds content.

ANNA QUINDLEN

Something like home that is
not home is to be desired; it is
found in the house of a friend.

SIR WILLIAM TEMPLE

We need old friends to help us
grow old and new friends to
help us stay young.

LETTY COTTIN POGREBIN

Each friend represents a world
in us, a world possibly not
born until they arrive, and it is
only by this meeting that a new
world is born.

ANAÏS NIN

Hold a true friend with both
your hands.

NIGERIAN PROVERB

The growth of true friendship
may be a lifelong affair.

SARAH ORNE JEWETT

Being a friend means master-
ing the art of timing.

GLORIA NAYLOR

There are no rules for friendship. It must be left to itself.
We cannot force it any more
than love.

WILLIAM HAZLITT

Love and friendship are the
discoveries of ourselves in
others, and our delight in the
recognition.

ALEXANDER SMITH

I can trust my friends. These people force me to examine, encourage me to grow.

CHER

Promises may get friends, but it is performance that must nurse and keep them.

OWEN FELTHAM

Friendship is a strong and habitual inclination in two persons to promote the good and happiness of one another.

EUSTACE BUDGELL

Never weary of making friends.

ASHER B. YEHIEL

A friend you have to buy won't be worth what you pay for him.

G. D. PRENTICE

I think this is the beginning of
a beautiful friendship.

SPOKEN BY HUMPHREY BOGART
TO CLAUDE RAINS,
CASABLANCA

True friends, like ivy
and the wall
Both stand together,
and together fall.

THOMAS CARLYLE

Friendship is the marriage of
the soul.

VOLTAIRE

Nobody sees a flower, really—
it is so small—we haven't
time, and to see takes time,
like to have a friend takes time.

GEORGIA O'KEEFFE

Friendship is a living thing that
must be nourished.

LINDA E. SHEPHERD

He who throws away a friend is
as bad as he who throws away
his life.

SOPHOCLES

Friendship is a single soul
dwelling in two bodies.

ARISTOTLE

Friendship's a noble name, 'tis
love refined.

SUSANNAH CENTLIVRE

Friendships, like marriage, are dependent on avoiding the unforgivable.

JOHN D. MACDONALD

Go often to the house of thy
friend; for weeds soon choke
up the unused path.

EDDA (SCANDINAVIAN MYTHOLOGY)

No distance of place or
lapse of time can lessen the
friendship of those who are
thoroughly persuaded of each
other's worth.

ROBERT SOUTHEY

Traveling in the company of
those we love is home in
motion.

LEIGH HUNT

Wherever you are it is your
own friends who make your
world.

WILLIAM JAMES

Be a friend to thyself, and others will be so too.

THOMAS FULLER

We never know the true value
of friends. While they live we
are too sensitive of their faults:
when we have lost them we
only see their virtues.

J. C. AND A. W. HARE

Friendship is the source of the
greatest pleasures, and without
friends even the most agree-
able pursuits become tedious.

ST. THOMAS AQUINAS

Friendship takes fear from the heart.

MAHABHARATA

What do we live for, if it is not to make life less difficult for each other?

GEORGE ELIOT

For believe me, in this world, which is ever slipping from under our feet, it is the prerogative of friendship to grow old with one's friends.

ARTHUR S. HARDY

22

Don't burn bridges. You'll be surprised how many times you have to cross the same river.

H. JACKSON BROWN

Sir, I look upon every day to be lost, in which I do not make a new acquaintance.

SAMUEL JOHNSON

There is nothing so great that I fear to do it for my friend; nothing so small that I will disdain to do it for him.

SIR PHILIP SIDNEY

No man is useless while he has
a friend.

ROBERT LOUIS STEVENSON

Forget your woes when you
see your friend.

PRISCIAN

Two persons cannot long be
friends if they cannot forgive
each other's little failings.

JEAN DE LA BRUYÈRE

It is chance that makes broth-
ers, but hearts that make
friends.

ANONYMOUS

When you know who his friend
is, you know who he is.

SENEGALESE PROVERB

Our friendships with one
another are the currency of
our lives.

TONI MORRISON

The man who treasures his
friends is usually solid gold
himself.

MARJORIE HOLMES

No man is the whole of
himself. His friends are the
rest of him.

GOOD LIFE ALMANAC

Nothing makes the earth seem so spacious as to have friends at a distance; they make the latitudes and the longitudes.

HENRY DAVID THOREAU

We have been together in sunshine and in shade.

CAROLINE E. S. NORTON

Friendship is the shadow of the evening, which strengthens with the setting sun of life.

JEAN DE LA FONTAINE

Be slow to fall into friendship;
but when thou art in, continue
firm and constant.

SOCRATES

All people have their fancies. . .
but I have a passion for
friends.

PLATO

It is not what you give your
friend, but what you are will-
ing to give him, that deter-
mines the quality of friendship.

MARY DIXON THAYER

There is in friendship something of all relations, and
something above them all. It is
the golden thread that ties the
heart of all the world.

JOHN EVELYN

What a thing friendship is—
World without end!

ROBERT BROWNING

But if the while I think on
    thee, dear friend,
All losses are restor'd and
    sorrows end.

WILLIAM SHAKESPEARE

True friendship is never
serene.

MARIE DE SÉVIGNÉ

The only good teachers for you
are those friends who love you,
who think you are interesting,
or very important, or wonder-
fully funny.

BRENDA UELAND

Good Words
Between Good Friends

I know what things are good:
friendship and work and
conversation.

RUPERT BROOKE

Friends put the entire world to
rights over a cup of tea and a
bun.

CHARLOTTE GRAY

I always felt that the great high privilege, relief and comfort of friendship was that one had to explain nothing.

KATHERINE MANSFIELD

A true test of friendship—to sit or walk with a friend for an hour in perfect silence without wearying of one another's company.

DINAH MULOCH CRAIK

Talking with one another is
loving one another.

KENYAN PROVERB

The proper office of a friend is
to side with you when you are
in the wrong. Nearly anybody
will side with you when you
are in the right.

MARK TWAIN

A friend is one before whom I
may think aloud.

RALPH WALDO EMERSON

A friend is a person with whom
you dare to be yourself.

PAM BROWN

I don't have to worry about
being misunderstood. When it
comes to knowing who I am,
she gets the big picture.

GAIL LOPATA LENNON

When friends stop being frank
and useful to each other, the
whole world loses some of its
radiance.

ANATOLE BROYARD

Are we not like two volumes of
one book?

MARCELINE DESBORDES-VALMORE

I talked to friends and found myself.

LOIS WYSE

I was successful because you believed in me.

ULYSSES S. GRANT

The love of our neighbor in all its fullness simply means being able to say to him, "What are you going through?"

SIMONE WEIL

It isn't so much what's on the table that matters, as what's on the chairs.

W. S. GILBERT

When two friends part they should lock up each other's secrets and exchange keys. The truly noble mind has no resentments.

DIOGENES

True friendship comes when
silence between two people is
comfortable.

DAVE TYSON GENTRY

Be not disturbed at being
misunderstood; be disturbed
rather at not being under-
standing.

CHINESE PROVERB

Some friends play at friendship
but a true friend sticks closer
than one's nearest kin.

PROVERBS 18:24 (NRSV)

Being with you is like walking
on a very clear morning—
definitely the sensation of
belonging.

E. B. White

Friends are the sunshine of life.

John Hay

She became for me an island of
light, fun, wisdom where I
could run with my discoveries
and torments and hopes at any
time of day and find welcome.

May Sarton

Friendship is the hardest thing
in the world to explain. It's not
something you learn in school.
But if you haven't learned the
meaning of friendship, you
really haven't learned any-
thing.

MUHAMMAD ALI

Never exaggerate your faults;
your friends will attend to that.

ROBERT C. EDWARDS

The Virtues
of a Friend

The ones that give, get back
in kind.

PAM DURBAN

Real friends are those who,
when you've made a fool of
yourself, don't feel that you've
done a permanent job.

ERWIN T. RANDALL

My best friend is the one who
brings out the best in me.

HENRY FORD

Don't expect your friends to
have better qualities than you
do—or fewer faults.

The beauty and loveliness of
friendship is too strong for
dim eyes.

HENRY FIELDING

A faithful friend is a strong
    defense;
And he that hath found him
    hath found a treasure.

LOUISA MAY ALCOTT

When the sun shines on you,
you see your friends. Friends
are the thermometers by which
one may judge the tempera-
ture of our fortunes.

MARGUERITE BLESSINGTON

You must act in your friend's interest whether it pleases him or not; the object of love is to serve, not to win.

WOODROW WILSON

We are not primarily put on earth to see through one another, but to see one another through.

PETER DE VRIES

One's friends are that part of
the human race with which
one can be human.

GEORGE SANTAYANA

Looking to the other for
inspiration, we went ahead
and learned what we needed
to know.

STACY ALLISON

Old friends are best. King
James us'd to call for his old
shoes, they were easiest for
his feet.

JOHN SELDEN

Today I have the possibility to
be open to the possibility that
someone who reaches out just
wants to be with *me*.

ANNE WILSON SCHAEF

Friends are needed both for
joy and for sorrow.

YIDDISH PROVERB

Who ceases to be a friend
never was one.

ANONYMOUS

True friendship is like sound
health; the value of it is seldom
known until it be lost.

CHARLES CALEB COLTON

54

A friend will prove himself in
time of trouble.

M. IBN EZRA

A friendless man is like a left
hand without a right.

HEBREW PROVERB

A friend is one who comes to
you when all others leave.

IZAAK WALTON

There is nothing final between
friends.

WILLIAM JENNINGS BRYAN

Give me one friend, just one,
    who meets
The needs of all my varying
    moods.

ESTHER M. CLARK

He who is true to one friend
thus proves himself worthy of
many.

ANONYMOUS

To friendship every burden's
light.

JOHN GAY

Happiness is perfume: you
can't pour it on somebody else
without getting a few drops on
yourself.

JAMES VAN DER ZEE

Every true friend is a glimpse
of God.

LUCY LARCOM

Friends—and I mean real
friends—reserve nothing;
The property of one belongs to
the other.

EURIPIDES

Spare me not because I am
your friend. For that very
reason spare me not.

SAMUEL RICHARDSON

Friendship is an affection of earth.

EDWARD BULWER-LYTTON

There is nothing meritorious but virtue and friendship.

ALEXANDER POPE

My friends are my heart and my ears.

MICHAEL JORDAN

A real friend is one who walks
in when the rest of the world
walks out.

WALTER WINCHELL

Friendship is the highest
degree of perfection in society.

MICHEL DE MONTAIGNE

Who seeks a friend without
fault remains without one.

TURKISH PROVERB

A Father's a Treasure; a
Brother's a Comfort; a Friend
is both.

BENJAMIN FRANKLIN

Under the magnetism of
friendship the modest man
becomes bold; the shy, confi-
dent; the lazy, active; or the
impetuous, prudent and
peaceful.

WILLIAM MAKEPEACE THACKERAY

The supreme happiness of life
is the conviction of being loved
for yourself, or, more correctly,
being loved in spite of yourself.

VICTOR HUGO

A true friend unbosoms freely,
advises justly, assists readily,
adventures boldly, talks all
patiently, defends courageous-
ly, and continues a friend
unchangeably.

WILLIAM PENN

Treat your friends as you do
your pictures, and place them
in their best light.

JENNIE JEROME CHURCHILL

The older a friend the better.

PLAUTUS

If I don't have friends, then I
ain't got nothin'.

BILLIE HOLIDAY